SMARTYpants
secrets

CONFIDENCE

It's NEEDED By ALL- Gaining It if You Don't Have It or Don't Have Enough; Keeping It if You Do

D.R. Martin, PhD*
(*Personal human Development)

SmartyPants Press
Falmouth, Maine 04105
www.SmartyPantsSecrets.com

ISBN 13: 978-1-943971-10-7
ISBN 10: 1943971102

Copyright 2016 D.R. Martin, PhD*
(*Personal human Development)

Disclaimer: This is an informational guide and is not intended as a substitute for legal or other professional services. Readers are urged to consult a variety of sources and educate themselves more fully about the designated topic. While every effort has been made to make this guide accurate, it may contain typographical and content errors. The information expressed herein is the sole researched and experienced opinion of the author(s), is not intended to reflect upon any particular person or company. The author(s) and publisher shall have no responsibility or liability with respect to any loss or damage caused, or alleged to be caused, by the information or application contained in this guide.

The SmartyPants Secrets Concept

A **SmartyPants Secret** is that **one piece of information** that you need to know to make every job a little bit, or maybe a lot, **easier**. Almost everything we do in life has a SmartyPants secret that to it, that knowing the "secret" would help tremendously in shortening the learning curve.

After experiencing many "a ha!" moments that were previous head bangers, I realized that there was a lot of grief – i.e. aggravation, wasted time, spent resources - that could have been saved if I had known to tap into the insider information that others had and I was lacking. A SmartyPants secret is that crucial bit of timely knowledge.

We all want a magic bullet answer that solves all of our problems in one fell swoop and makes everything go perfectly well, preferably in record time! We want that magic to happen right NOW, to be easily done, and to be preferably cheap, or at least not at great expense. There are a lot of demands on our unattainable magic ☺

For example, one day I looked at my face and damn if I didn't see a "sun spot" (nastily also called a "liver" spot) marring the surface of my otherwise smooth face on the right lower cheek. I scheduled an appointment at the dermatologist to verify the find and see if it could be lasered off. She sent me to an aesthetician who gave me some key information that made a huge difference in my decision of what to do next.

I was told that my even slightly darker (Asian) skin carries more pigment than Caucasian skin obviously. But what's not obvious is the way the body works, specifically the way the skin works, which is that when you wound the skin's surface, which laser surgery would certainly do, extra pigments rush to the spot to heal it (the "job" of pigment is to protect the underlying cells). The net result is that non-Caucasian skin heals into darker scabs and scars. (I have noticed this phenomena before but never made a direct connection.) Why then would I ever choose to have laser surgery on my face to remove a mark only to end up with an even darker mark? Yikes!

Obviously I wouldn't, but without this specialized knowledge about different results with different skin types, that even the dermatologist didn't know (yes, she was the recommender of the laser surgery option) I would've made a poor decision, with permanent negative results. A SmartyPants timely secret to the rescue!

Experts, who have hours of experience doing what the newbie is attempting to do, have expert knowledge, which may not be so secret, but it is **key information** that the novice greatly needs.

If you've ever struggled with something then learned the 'something' afterwards that caused you to say to yourself or to say aloud, "*Well, **if I only known THAT before I did this**, it would've made a world of difference!*" then you just learned a SmartyPants secret - the hard way.

The short SmartyPants Secrets books give you the secret that you need on a given topic, the most important piece of information that makes the greatest difference between easier success and hard-fought failure.

When I was young there was a professor at Cornell University, which in his obituary listed him as "***the last man to know everything***." I was taken by the concept of anyone knowing everything there is to know contained in one brain. Oh, to have such a mind!

But **to know everything**, logical facts and figures, and **to be able to do everything** are **two different things**. Brain power doesn't equal skill and expertise.

Today that one brain that knows everything is the Internet. There is so much information today available on the Internet; we can all be like that professor at Cornell and have access to all knowledge at the click of our fingertips.

More knowledge than we could ever consume - **who has time** to go through it all? Most of the time **what you really want is to know is the crux of the subject** on hand, not the whole litany of everything imaginable that is available to know.

Tell me just what I need to know! (and I likely don't know what specific knowledge to ask for). It's literally impossible to know what you don't know. Let the expertise of knowledgeable others guide you.

If you are new to a topic the **SmartyPants secret can save you time and effort**, which are important to your success. Not a complete course on the topic, which you can certainly get elsewhere, the SmartyPants secrets concept is primarily to help you **not miss the key information needed for success**.

The building block of knowledge that the foundation rests upon; the Keystone or cornerstone knowledge makes a critical difference, especially when that knowledge that you do have, or think you have, is **faulty, incomplete or missing** entirely.

The concept of **social proof** states that when we have no prior experience in a given situation we rely on **others to show us the way**. We believe that lacking personal knowledge, that their situation is similar to our situation, and therefore what worked for them has a high probability of working for us.

We quiz others about our shared circumstances around the situation to verify that their solution is a good one. Plus, we think: *there's nothing to lose in trying since I don't have a better answer.*

Then when what worked for another doesn't happen to work for us, we are reminded that **we are all different people**, with different variables that impact success or failure. Some solutions to problems are hit or miss depending on who we are. And sometimes success depends on having and following the right key knowledge.

Solving problems is not the complete SmartyPants concept, although SmartyPants secrets can indeed offer real help for real problems. Rather the full concept is that having that key knowledge piece makes efforts easier and successful quicker; hopefully **avoiding having the problem in the first place**. We do anything in life because we have a goal to achieve. Reaching that goal successfully, quickly and easier than without knowing the SmartPants secret is the SmartyPants concept.

And because **all SmartyPants secrets have a physiological root**, grounded in our shared human biology, every SmartyPants secret is valid for everyone, no matter who you are. While we are all uniquely different from each other, we have a **common biology** consisting of inherited traits that stretch back to the Neanderthal era.

Applying a SmartyPants secret **will work for you no matter who you are**. And in our busy world, who doesn't want to save time and know the SmartyPants secret to anything?

Why ever risk hindering easier success by not knowing the core success secret?

CONFIDENCE

Gaining & Keeping What Everyone Wants & Many Lack Enough Of

Much has been written on the subject of confidence, because it is perennially needed by most all. The subject is not what confidence is – we all know that – it's primarily *about how to gain and keep confidence* throughout the many situations in life that happen best when confidence is high.

SITUATIONAL NEEDS

Job interviews - you need to present, and impress at your best – and quickly!

Meeting an important person - *job*

importance (the big big boss is coming to the office), *personal importance* (big blind date; meeting the parents) – you not only want, **you need to be liked, respected and memorable** by Mr. Bigwig, by your date... please, bring on the confidence!

Making a big presentation in front of a

large or small group; you're well prepared, well-practiced, and well versed with the material and the audience - now your confidence just needs to hold through the **familiar opening jitters** as you approach the podium.

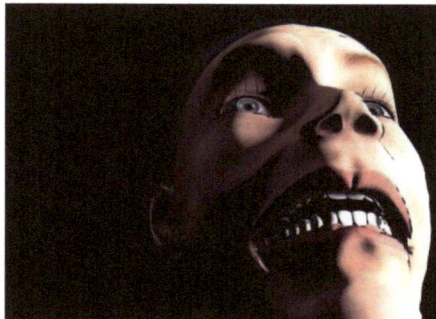

Giving a speech (*eulogy; award acceptance; motivating the troops*) – you might rather face a torture session, or maybe this is a torture session, than give this speech, but you're stuck and have to **face this fear**.

Your meager social life requires reserved-quiet-you to go out in public every so often, and 'perform' with small groups of others; interact with other people, some of who are familiar and some who are not as familiar.

Oh, the inane rituals of making small talk, engaging in mild banter, and basic showings of having a 'good time'. A heavy dose of social confidence, which doesn't come easily for you, would come in handy right about now.

Wouldn't it be simply lovely if confidence was as easily available as turning on a spigot, so you could just grab a big drink of it whenever you wanted some! Maybe there is such a thing...*read on*.

Where Does Confidence Come From?

Confidence comes from having **supreme comfort with all aspects of who you are**.

Situational confidence can change with different environmental conditions, but basic self-confidence, once developed and securely establish, once firmly OWNED, can be maintained for a lifetime.

Age and experience bring confidence. Not all the time, and not a guarantee for everyone, but much of the time this is the case for most people. The older we get, the wiser we usually become; then we don't allow our once shaky confidence to erode so quickly, if at all.

This Takes Confidence Away

FDR said it best, "You have nothing to fear but fear itself" – **fear** takes away confidence. *Fear of failure, fear of rejection, fear of looking bad, fear of not being liked, fear of making a mistake.* Very real fears, founded in very real concerns, dealing with very real emotions.

To have confidence, you must face your fears head on, and dispel them with experience ("I lived through this horror show; I can take whatever else is thrown my way"), preparation (know your subject and your audience well), and not being afraid of being wrong. Confidence lets you know that it's really ok to make a mistake.

Talking about your fears, communicating with others what you fear, also helps to eliminate it.

ME WORRY?

The face of confidence!

Childhood Issues Become Adult Issues

The formative years, primarily up to age 12, form much of who we become for life. We are necessarily heavily influenced by experiences and treatment by interactions with peers and other adults.

The **child who is bullied**, the child who bullies, and the child who watches bullying happening are all impacted in their confidence development.

The **child who is different** (size, weight, glasses, race, religion, dress, hair, freckles, etc.) may rail against the injustice of circumstances that is beyond their control, but distinctly feels the effects on their confidence in the reactions of others.

Our childhood reactions to impacting experiences of daily life, which are also beyond a child's ability to control or fully understand, forms the backbone of our adult confidence.

Fight, Flight, or Freeze

The primary reactions to any alarming experience – fight, flight or freeze – can become ingrained and solidified by adulthood.

Fight – subconscious: *I am not going to allow this negative experience to make me weak and vulnerable to hurt.* A tough exterior shell can be built that may develop into true confidence, or alternately can hide deep anxiety under a good show of tough bravado.

Flight – subconscious: *I am overcome by negative experience that feels unrelenting and overwhelming, consuming my world and thoughts of self-worth*. Depression, bouts of anxiety, panic attacks and other negative emotions allow the mind to take control of the physical body.

Freeze – subconscious: *If I ignore negative experience and don't think about them, they will go away.* Letting things roll is really the healthiest approach. Knowing deep down that it's not your fault, and not taking it personally where it effects your psyche is the luck of a carefree childhood.

GAINING CONFIDENCE - It's Really Not That Hard

FACTOR: *Thorough Preparation*

When thoroughly prepared, having taken the time to think through all aspects of the situation and determining in advance the **if-that-then-this actions** really helps to develop and keep situational confidence.

Physical space location considerations, environmental considerations, and mental preparation all factor into confidence.

FACTOR: *Practice, Practice, Practice*

Confidence comes from being well versed in the material, knowing it well and practicing the delivery; not practicing so that you won't get it wrong, rather confidence is not being afraid of being wrong.

Without the feeling of having a **solid base to stand on that practice gives**, situational confidence can easily be thrown off balance.

FACTOR: *Self-Talk Pronouns Matter*

Talk to yourself, psyche yourself up in the **3rd person – "you" or refer to yourself by your first name – makes you more confident** than using 1st person language of "I" or "me".

Distancing yourself from your fears by referring to yourself in your self-talk in the 3rd person helps you to see yourself from outside of yourself. With this outside perspective you can't see what everyone else sees – a person who is well prepared, confident, capable.

X, ME --> YOU

FACTOR: *Mind-Body Connection*

The power of how the mind and body are symbiotically connected and the 2-way influence they share is not to be discounted. **Know it and become it** is real, as is *do it and become it*.

You want confidence, right before the big situation presents? Let your body tell your mind that you have confidence and it will happen. Really.

Words of confidence, which are in your head, do not necessarily utilize the mind-body connection. Repeating a mantra over and over internally or aloud – *I am confidence, I am confident, I am supremely confident* – doesn't hurt, but still doesn't go far enough.

To employ the mind-body connection concept, you need to put the body in a confident position, call the **Power Pose**, which tells the mind that the body is confident, therefore it must be so.

Looking like Wonder Woman or Victorious Warrior, with legs firmly planted and hands on hips, or arms and hands raised in victory is the body position of confidence.

But also **key is to hold the pose** (in private) for enough time – 90 seconds is good – so the mind can assimilate and process the body's message, and follow suit. A common mistake is to strike the pose, then not to hold it long enough, then wonder why it didn't work...!

FACTOR: *Body Language*

Body language is a big part of communicating confidence to others. The primary way confidence is shown is **by taking up space** – the more space a person occupies, the more confident they not only appear to others, but the more confident they actually are.

Arms open, outstretched, draping over the chair beside you; legs open and forward, not held tightly underneath you; fingers splayed and spread apart – these are all **body language signs of high confidence.**

FACTOR: *Handshake*

Ready with that great handshake, which **telegraphs so much, on both sides**. How does the other person feel about you and the pending interaction with you? If you knew that answer, would it have a strong effect on your confidence? Can you influence how the other person feels about you with your own good handshake, giving your confidence a nice boost? Sure you can!

You've heard that a good handshake is nice and firm, palm to palm, and web to web. Not too firm (you don't want to crush the other person's hand with an overly showy display of strength) and definitely not too weak. To enhance the handshake experience, as you grip the other person's hand extend your index finger out to cover their wrist pulse. This subtle change **feels great to the other person**, without their knowing why.

Additionally if you reach out with your palm facing upward, giving the other person the 'upper hand', and then while shaking you pull their hand and arm in towards your abdomen slightly, giving them 'access' to your most vulnerable area, **subconsciously you've made them feel very strong.**

This feeling of strength makes them like you more, having experienced this fabulous handshake, and the person doesn't even know why. Putting the other person in such a good space should **ramp up your confidence** that the upcoming interaction is starting out on very positive footing.

FACTOR: *Posture*

Posture and gait are primary indicators of a person's confidence level. Walking around quickly, with a relaxed but upright stride, and standing with that same good posture exudes confidence.

It's not about walking so quickly that no one else can keep up. But it is about walking with purpose and focus; not dawdling or strolling along too leisurely.

Sitting and standing with shoulders back, not hunched up and not sagging, with the back firm but not ramrod military straight, connotes confidence. Mother was right when she badgered you to sit up straight and not slouch.

Posture is a habit, which can be good or can be bad. The **habit of good posture** is part of the habit of confidence.

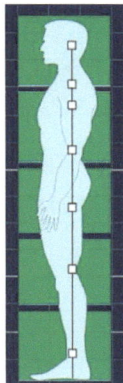

FACTOR: *Create a Confidence Trigger*

Wouldn't it be great to have a private button that you could push whenever you needed confidence, available to you for any situation that comes up? Well you can create such a trigger, a cue that you fire off when you need it, delivering to you the needed confidence (if it's properly created) on the spot!

To create a confidence trigger in advance, find a quiet time to sit with yourself. Close your eyes and recall an experience when you were at your most confident. Re-live that experience in your mind's eye, slowly and in full color, start at the beginning and then recall all the details of what happened, bit by bit.

When you get to the part in the memory where you are re-living the moment at the height of confidence, create your own personal trigger incorporating a movement (e.g. run your right index finger along your right jawline), a visual sign (e.g. 'thumbs up' with your left thumb), and a sound (e.g. say the word "yeah!"). Repeat this trigger creation process several times with the same memory to anchor in the trigger.

When you need confidence, if you've created the trigger properly, you should be able to fire it off by simply start with the designated movement, then look at the visual sign and hear or say the designated word. The high confidence should flow through your body and be available for your immediate use.

Training your brain to deliver needed resources, that it holds embedded in memory, on command when you need them is a good skill in self-control.

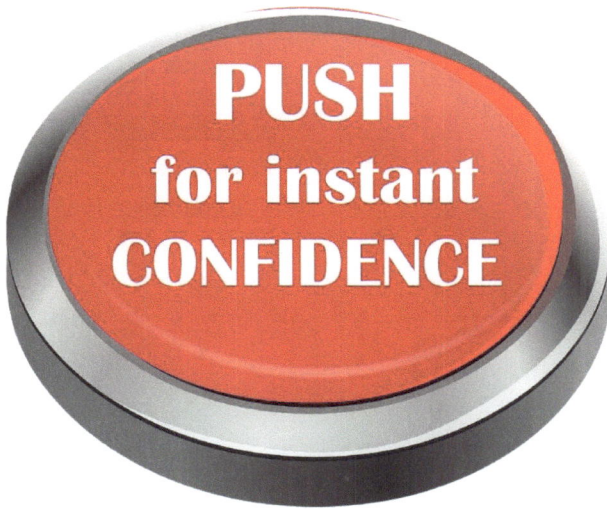

COMMAND PRESENCE

Command presence is what people with supreme confidence have, and what aspiring leaders and executives want. Those with command presence **own the room when they walk in,** in an assertive comfortingly confident way. They exude confidence, expertise, authority over the environment.

FACTOR: *Stand facing the other person, right eyes aligned*

This is especially important when standing man-to-man, because males standing face-to-face, without being slightly off center (i.e. right eyes aligned) is highly confrontational, which you don't want. A confident command presence is **assertive, not aggressive**.

The right eye alignment also puts you in the best position for the other person to **view you most favorably**. This of course, helps your confidence!

FACTOR: *Stand in closer*

Confident people take advantage of a **tighter space bubble that others allow them.** The invisible but real space zones everyone has around them are the **comfort zones** based on how well we know and how much we like the other person.

Because **confident people are likable** – we like confidence and confident people, *hoping that some of their confidence will rub off* on us – we **give them greater latitude** to move in on our tighter space bubbles, even if we don't know them that well (which we want to do).

To develop command presence, show confidence by standing a bit closer (without offending please) and gauge the effect on others.

OK, that's perhaps a bit TOO close!

FACTOR: *Maintain a Steady Gaze*

To have command presence, master the art of maintaining good eye contact while conversing with others. Looking interested and focusing solely on the other person is a great way to build rapport. Everyone loves to have another person's wholly undivided attention for any period of time.

The rule of thumb is to look at the person 70% of the time while they are talking, and 40% of the time while you are talking. Anything more is too steady a gaze (bordering on creepy); anything less feels like a lack of good engagement and not committed to the conversation (mind is elsewhere/wandering).

The sweet spot to look, if you have trouble stare into their eyes for so long, is to gaze at that 'third eye' triangle right between the eyes. They will think you are looking right into their eyes.

FACTOR: *Hands should be openly displayed, palms open*

An open hand is the top sign up nothing to hide, full honesty, and integrity. So no hands in pockets, or hiding behind your back, or tucked into your crossed arms.

To have the confidence of a command presence is to maintain those hands out in the open on full display.

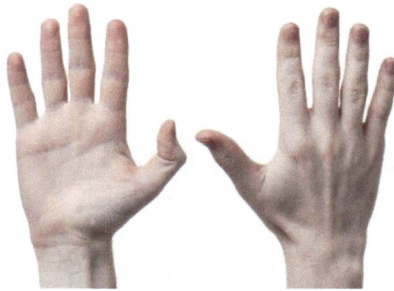

FACTOR: *Minimal Movement*

A confident person doesn't have an excess of unnecessary movement, which is more representative of a nervous person with hyper energy and agitation.

This is not to say that enthusiasm, passion, and an energetic display must be quelled or toned down. On the contrary, these desirable qualities are magnetic to others.

What needs to be kept to a minimum are the nervous habits involving unneeded movement like jiggling of change in a pocket, clicking a handheld pen, even a continual but unknown bobbing or shaking of the head. Minimize these bad habits of excessive movement to display greater confidence.

FACTOR: *Gesture in the Power Sphere*

Keep hand gestures within the imaginary beach ball-sized area between the chest and the navel, the 'power sphere'.

To gesture is important, to animate the passion felt, but wild large gestures do not look confident and small tight gestures lacked proper energy. Staying in the power sphere with hand gestures is the way to go for command presence and for confidence.

Holding on to Confidence When Gained

Now that you have confidence, how to hold onto it? Can it be **maintained** for as long as you need it? How do you keep from being **thrown off your game and losing your confidence** when you are in the middle of the situation?

FACTOR: *Really Understand the Audience*

Who is in front of you? How well do you really know them? If not the person personally, how well do you know their group cohort? The **better your understanding of who they are**, what they're going through, their issues of concern, their enjoyments, even on a general level (although more specific is much better), the better chance you have of maintaining your confidence.

"I know you guys, I'm one of you" should be the impression that you're trying to get across. We like other people who are like us. If you know the audience, if you can relate strongly to what's important to them, then you are in a

good position to be likable and to deliver your expertise with confidence.

This is in your wheelhouse – and if it's not, then make it so, or your confidence will be easily eroded.

FACTOR: *Use Humor, Clever Wit*

Make 'em laugh, not necessarily with jokes if you are not a professional comedian (amateurs tend to bring out more groans than laughs), but with clever wit or self-deprecating humor.

When we can laugh at ourselves, others relate to the foible and laugh along in agreement. This **upfront agreement through laughter is extremely persuasive** and great for maintaining confidence

Making others laugh makes you more likable. Laughter releases endorphins, the body's feel-good chemical; everyone likes to feel good, so everyone likes to laugh. When you are the catalyst for people to laugh, you are sought out company.

FACTOR: *Stand Ahead, Take the Lead*

A leader must have followers to lead. If you have and hold confidence, **others who are drawn to your confidence** and to the cause that you represent, will follow your confidence gladly.

Many are looking for reason to believe, to link with a cause that is greater than themselves, to be part of something that they can't achieve on their own. It is the quest for immortality on a bigger stage, to **align with a greater purpose**.

The leader with confidence stands apart in their belief, which can accomplish amazing things when the cause is for the greater good.

FACTOR: *Tell Relatable Stories*

Everyone loves a good story, so everyone loves a good storyteller. A good story is memorable and repeated. A good story is **concrete and full of detailed imagery**. A good story paints a picture with words.

We love to **root the underdog**. We love to play the hero by following on the hero's journey with them, learning their lessons and experiencing their ahas; the story format allows this enjoyable vicarious experience, as long as the hero and the story are **relatable and relevant.**

Develop and tell stories that **create meaningful connections** between the listener's life and the protagonist of the story. Your audience will absorb, retain, and repeat your point, if the story is well told.

You say you're not a good storyteller? Develop this skill with practice, practice, practice (for good confidence) and it will pay you many dividends.

FACTOR: *Connect and Engage*

Be authentic. No one wants to be around or has any confidence in an inauthentic, disingenuous person. Engage others in an authentic way – ask for their help or assistance that is truly needed. Ask for their support and give yours in return. **An engaged person is motivated** to maintain their involvement.

Smile! A lot. **Genuine smiling**, not that fake pasty stuff (everyone knows the difference, no one is fooled); real smiles reach all the way up to the eyes. Even **smile when no one is looking**, which will serve to lift your mood and make you feel more confident. It is impossible to maintain a bad mood while genuinely smiling; the mind-body connection works well.

Smiles release endorphins, across both the smiler and the smile. When you give a smile, you get a smile back (our mirror neurons make smiling back almost automatic behavior) – it's a win-win for both sides! It also **ups the likability quotient** – we like people who make us smile. We like confident smiling people :)

The SmartyPants Secret on:
CONFIDENCE:

You choose your perspective – you can decide how you WANT to look at a situation, which gives you confidence (or takes it away!)

Knowing you have the power to choose, that exercising the power in the moment is the secret to having and keeping confidence.

Recognize that confidence is totally subjective and is a resource (or hindrance) under your full control, to exercise at will.

BOOK BUYER BONUS

As a thank you to buyers, there is an additional free resource available only to book buyers. Did you get yours? If you missed it, go to www.SmartyPantsSecrets.com/bookbonus .

It's has additional valuable content and is free to book buyers, so don't miss out on getting yours!

BOOK RESOURCE

This SmartyPants Secrets book has a companion resource on the topic that may be of interest. The resource for this Confidence Book is **100% natural organic *Confidence in a Bottle*, to support situational confidence issues.**

Confidence in a Bottle not only works to support own confidence, it also makes a lovely gift for others you care about that may be experiencing confidence impairment issues.

For ordering and other information on this and other SmartyPants Secrets support products, visit the website at www.SmartyPantsSecrets.com/resources .

ABOUT

I am DR Martin, PhD* (*Personal human
Development expertise) – Dolley Rapoport
Martin. I took Dolley as my first name* in
honor of the great First Lady Dolley Madison,
whom I admire for her heroic actions in the
White House during very turbulent times.

I took Rapoport as a middle name* in honor of
Ingeborg Rapoport, who at age 103, is the
oldest person to be awarded a Doctorate;
finally getting the recognition due her from 77
years prior in Nazi Germany, unfairly denied
her due to her Jewish roots. There is so much
injustice in the world; it is an honor to
recognize her achievement by taking her
name. [*The selecting of one's name is an important
exercise, since names are so personal and tied to identity. Yet
most of us go through life with a name not of our choosing.
Check out the SmartyPants Secret book NAMES.]

I have studied every communication subject
for more than a decade, acquiring a large body
of knowledge. I, perhaps like you, am a
voracious reader and learner. My other
strength is that I retain much of what I learn,
so I can then compile the knowledge on a

variety of subjects into a concise format, making the books that I author a shortcut on the best knowledge available. This saves you from going through all the data looking for the kernel that makes the greatest difference in success, the SmartyPants secret on a given topic.

I also have a mind that is ever curious about so many topics. I have earned multiple expert designations (education certified English teacher, Real Estate Broker, Stock Broker series 7, series 6, series, Certified Financial Manager, Insurance producer certified, Coach University) and held high level positions in business – large corporate entities, privately held companies, non-profit organizations, and startups – and have volunteered extensively, holding executive positions at the local, district and national levels. So I've been around the block more than once, on more than one topic.

Due to my research and experience, I have logged the perquisite time to carry the title of expert, giving myself an honorary PhD in the expertise area of communication, Personal human Development. I am passionate about sharing the knowledge that I have gained with you, in bite-size pieces.

And when a certain topic is not in my field of expertise, I find an expert with deep expertise in the field who has the knowledge that I seek. I then ask numerous in-depth questions of the expert to get to the gist, learn the SmartyPants Secret, to then pass the knowledge on in a book on the subject.

SMARTYpants
secrets

For other titles and additional resources, visit www.SmartyPantsSecrets.com

All book titles at www.amazon.com/-/e/B018HA35I8

Watch for content clips and helpful technique tips on a variety of topics coming soon at www.youtube.com/c/smartypantssecrets

Contact: Info@SmartyPantsSecrets.com

www.ingramcontent.com/pod-product-compliance
Lightning Source LLC
Chambersburg PA
CBHW041227270326
41934CB00001B/27